INSIDE A TEENAGER'S BRAIN

Dreams Do Come True, As Long As You Know Your Worth.

Bhavika Maye

BookLeaf Publishing

India | USA | UK

Made with ❤ on the BookLeaf Publishing Platform
www.bookleafpub.in
www.bookleafpub.com

Dedication

To my mother and sister, thank you for always being there for me, understanding me, and my choices. I don't know what I would do without you. Love you.
To avva, I miss you.
To friends who believed in me.

Preface

"Inside a teenager's brain" — this book will acknowledge your feelings, for the positivity that one might dwell in, isn't always the best way to be heard. As you read, I hope you embrace emotions, both good and bad,

because everything leads to growth, as a person. I have written about my experiences and my beliefs, wishing it resonates with many. While writing this, I'm hoping this book, which is a part of me, reaches those who feel like no one is listening. Yes, one must hope that things will always get better, but this does not mean we neglect our emotions that raise doubt and fear, as we are humans— we feel and it is okay, to feel. We shall be optimistic but also corroborate the feeling of uncertainty, as long as we don't stop dreaming and believing that things will change for the better and they will. I want this part of me, my poems, to empathise with my readers' pain and reassure their beliefs. I know that a lot of you are hurting, I want this book to tell you that it'll be okay and that you all will achieve what you are determined to achieve. Life is not all that bad, there's a lot to be happy about and that is what this book is about, it is what it says: dreams do come true, regardless of the obstacles we might face in the way. Work hard and believe that you can, and nothing can stop you from turning your dreams into reality. Effort and faith— and you will be fine.

Acknowledgements

Grateful to the occasion of being alive.
Grateful to nature.
Grateful to many.
To the reason I have this opportunity to debut as an
author: BookLeaf Publishing.
To my readers, I genuinely hope my poems make you
happy, or help you cry if you've been numb— so you can
be happy again. The destination is happiness.
And to my father, thank you for your financial support.

1. Love

Love, is what obsession is not.
Love, is not wanting them
Love, is wanting them to be happy,
regardless of whether there is your presence— in that
happiness.
Love, is being around them, which emanates comfort and
the utmost joy for you.

Love, is being able to be vulnerable around them,
knowing you can cry,
knowing you can laugh,
knowing you can open up,
and so can they, when they're around you.

Love is warmth
Love is angst
Love is emptiness
Love is fulfillment
Love is many things.

2. They bloom, darkly.

The flower blooms,
but can you see it all?
A part lies outside,
amongst everything and everyone.
The other dwells in darkness,
this half of it— is it blooming?

They hear this,
ask if I'm okay.
Why didn't you say so earlier?
I'd be deemed hideous,
too young to suffer.

It's okay,
for it is not validation I seek,
but mere empathy that I crave.

Trailed too far, I did.
Do I know?
I just hope the flower's okay.

3. The Sky

We rush, "We need to catch the sunset", we scream.
We arrive, I gaze.
It wasn't sunset
The moon was rising
And suddenly,
I'm all alone, inside my head
At peace.
Why aren't humans as quiet as the sky? I think to myself
Why aren't humans as accepting as the sky? Longingly I
wonder
There are people as serene as the sky,
and just as accepting.
There are people as serene as the sky,
and they aren't as accepting— as the sky is.

But it's okay, people are different.
So is the sky every day.
Again, suddenly, I am not just, "I"
"We", exist again.
I look at them,
It's okay, I tell myself.
They're different,
but they're my people.

Humans I dread
Humans I yearn
Still human.

It's night
It will be morning again
The sky stays.

4. Am I Allowed To Grow Up?

I want something, I'm a child
I mess up, I'm an adult
I want solitude, I'm a child
I fail, I'm an adult

I am immature so I am an adult
I am irresponsible so I am an adult
I am tired so I am an adult
I want help so I am an adult
I cry so I am an adult

I want to choose so I am a child
I want privacy so I am a child

My space, where?
He screamed,
"It's my house, I paid for it"
The thumping door made me ponder,
"But is it home?"
My space, where?

Am I allowed to grow up?
I am a child.

I don't want to grow up!
I am an adult.

5. Petrichor

"Clubhouse table?"—she asked
I cut the call
It wasn't raining.

I head down to the table
She was already there
"You're late"—said she
I got déjà vu
Me and late
All so real.

We take rounds
"Wanna go to the park?"—she asked.
We're swinging
Suddenly we're on the sand
Our sleeves are rolled up
The water bottle is empty
The sand is not dry, anymore
It still isn't raining
Our hands, now coated with wet sand
We hold it up to our noses
It smells like rain; we say to each other,
Giggling.
Pluviophiles, were we?

It wasn't raining
But it was— for us.

We did this often since then
It's been a while
I miss you
I wanna create fake petrichor with you— again.

P.S. You will always be my petrichor girl.

6. Ropes

She's free
She looks free
She acts free

But she's tied within,
with ropes.
Ropes she can't talk about
Ropes that are hidden
These ropes are visible,
but she makes them invisible,
every day.

She wants not the scarf,
no more.
Ropes she wasn't born with.
Ropes so unfamiliar,
now more familiar than ever.
Ropes now ploughing into her skin, she bleeds.
Ropes she didn't know would stay
Ropes she didn't know of.
How long does she have to wait?
So she can remove the scarf
So the ropes can be gone
So the ropes can actually be— invisible.

But she waits, for there lies a rope-free future for her.
She waits because she believes.
Because when the ropes are gone, she can indulge in a
scarf-free life.

Invisibility,
that rids so many, of their ropes.
Many whose scarves aren't enough,
for their ropes are far too visible,
nevertheless the vastness of the scarf.

Believing might not rid the ropes, but not believing will
not make her rope-free either.
She believes, and the ropes get closer to not existing.
She will only hurt more if she doesn't believe.
So, she believes.
She will be free.

Poet's note:
This is for all, regardless of physical or emotional ropes;
visible or invisible ropes. I dedicate this to not just
myself, but especially acid attack victims, burn victims,
abuse victims and anyone else who has had to suffer
silently. There are ropes that show, ropes that are

intuitively hidden and there are ropes that do not show,
so be kind.

11

7. She's there

There she was,
There was the newspaper
There was the spectacles' case

The hugs, every Saturday.
Your smile, when we walked in
And there you were, sipping on tea.

We sat down,
The newspaper noise, now no more.
The television muted, as you asked, "Did you eat?"
We said, "yes", but you headed to the kitchen anyway.

You aren't in the kitchen anymore
Your chair is empty, no walking stick next to it
I miss the newspaper noise, I miss the hugs
I miss your smell
I miss you.
I miss your bed, that we all laid on.
The bed that was free real estate, for every child in our
family.
The cocoa vaseline by your bed, that I would steal a
dollop of, every time I was there.
The square shaped mirror right next to it.

I can't help thinking,
Should I have been there more than I was?
Maybe I should've,
But I know,
That you were there for me,
More than I ever needed.
Sometimes, it makes me angry
That you were taken away, farther than I could hug you.
But I sleep in peace,
Knowing you're happier there.
Away from this ugly world.

There you are, in heaven.
I hope there are newspapers in heaven.
You are there.

8. House or Home?

Home did exist,
I was too young to remember.

I wanna go home, I said.
I got home,
What are you doing with your life! They screamed.
I'm trying, I said.
Where? They asked.
I go out,
Focus! They said.
I wanna go home, I said.

I will try today, I told myself.
I got home,
When will you do something about your future, they
screamed.
I break, I forget to try.
They say I pretend to be broken,
Apparently, I voluntarily bawl my eyes out till my gut
wrenches and my chest churns,
All so I could not try?
Valid observation,
It all obviously adds up.

Why are you broken? You are young.
Carry yourself as an adult would, they said.

I try, I fail.
It's okay, she said.
I fail and I fail again,
It's okay, she said.
I fail, I breathe for a while.
When will you start trying again, they asked.

I go out.
I wanna go home.
I get home.
A loop is what it was.
A loop that would eventually untangle and end.

They want to help me.
I know, I whisper to myself.
But is this the way?
I will get us back home one day, I promise myself.
I will not disappoint them,
More so, myself.

I don't feel at home anymore,
I'm at my house,
When will I get home?

I'm at home,
My brain raids my mood with, "I wanna go home"
I do want to go home

I live inside my bedroom, gladly.
I feel estranged from my living room
Now, more a lobby
As I spend days on end fantasising, to be alone in it,
So that it no more is a lobby.
I feel astray,
When can I go back home?

Open doors— they scare me.
Why?
It's the closest I can get to not being micromanaged
But they accuse me of hiding something
Because I'm still a baby
A baby they don't trust
A baby they overbear
A baby they have expectations from
A baby who must listen
A baby whom they don't listen to, only hear.
A baby who would care for herself if she wasn't pestered
about it
A baby whose mistakes are not the parents' fault
A baby whose work seems to go in vain as they steal
credit and abscond

Are parents kleptomaniacs?

I miss home
From when I was a baby.

9. Flower

Butterflies, they rest on you.
They rest on flowers.

You're rested upon,
by them, the butterflies.
What you are,
is what you're worth, a flower that stays.

You bloom, you wither.
More of you blooms, yet again.
You never die,
for you always get back up, mostly when I need nectar.
Thank you, for being my flower.

A flower that bloomed infinitely,
after infinite withers.
She was mine,
while I rested.
After my wings scabbed,
she told me I could fly again,
while the chameleon heard,
and didn't listen.
He chose not to ever listen
because that would lead to him understanding,

and that would never happen.
As he camouflaged based on his brothers' opinions,
and tattled to his friends,
loudly, in our forest.

I've learnt so far,
to stick to my flower and her daughter.
I will be their flower,
when they're butterflies who need to rest.
To amma,
I can be your flower too.

10. Let me...

I was barely seven,
I am seventeen as I write this,
I still resent you.

Ballet?
Guitar?
Badminton?
Swimming?
Science.

Listening, was he?
Was not.

Hurting, I was.
I was.

His words ring in my ear,
Echo into my heart and infest my brain.
"You're not capable of anything, it seems to me"
"Wake up!"— he screams at five in the morning
My burning eyes rely on my ears,
"You can't even wake up, you can't achieve anything"
Because that's all a 17 year old dreams of hearing,
Early in the morning.

I tell him I would like to study what I like,
"You can't achieve anything I guess"— he nonchalantly
replies.
I heard everything he said,
But I also listened.

Your daughter is trying to tell you something
Why won't you listen?
Let me,
Please.
You hear but you don't listen
You listen when I screech, but you don't understand.

You earn,
And for that I am grateful.
You earn money,
And you earn money
And you earn money
And you earn money
And money.

The shelter you provide and more,
I indulge,
In its physical comfort

But what about it, emotionally?
When can I ever have that?

What if the emotional pain infected my physical
comfort?
As it ate me up, not being able to stay just inside
anymore?

I am glad I had mom.
She was there for me,
In every way,
Understood me,
Understood what would make me happy,
But you don't let her help me either.
Your other daughter,
She wants me to be secure,
Just as you do,
But she understands my choice of risk.
To achieve, you have to try.
To try,
You have to risk,
I want to achieve,
So I want to try,
So I need to risk.

Why don't you care about what makes me happy?
I am writing
But it appears as though,
I am ranting
Maybe I am.

I will do what makes me happy
I will take risks
For I seek happiness
Just as much as you seek security for me
I need to prioritize myself,
To be happy.

To daddy,
I don't have it in me to allow you to keep hurting me
anymore.
I've had it.

11. Her, Moon & Sun

New place
New smell
New people
Cowardly as it sounds,
I condemn unfamiliarity,
as it fuels my anxiety,
and the voices get louder.

The door I pulled,
showed me her,
the girl in green.
She had that smile,
smile so adorable,
I wanted to put her in my pocket.

Can I sit here?
Yes, she gleefully replied as she moved her bag.
We connect,
as though the connection were lost before.
We like—
The same music
The same people
The same new language
We just agreed.

Most significantly,
we loved English.
Our heads snapped to look at each other,
whenever, all the time.
we just made sense.

We got each other
We got the difference between enunciation and
pronunciation
We got the difference between its and it's
We got the difference between your and you're
We got why the smell of books was ethereal.
I told her I loved the moon and the sun,
she understood that while looked down upon,
there was nothing wrong as it was love, regardless.
We get that it doesn't come as a choice,
if you love the moon and the sun,
you can't change it.
We need both darkness and light,
both the moon and the sun,
yet we degrade each other in this world,
purely based on love?
Inhumane much?
It is compelling when we,
as humans,
find it in us to accept.

First week of college,
I saw everyone rummaging through the classroom,
eating during the break,
until I couldn't see anymore,
eyes welled up,
chest too tight,
forgot how to breathe,
all a blur.
She smiles at me—
Five things you can see
Four things you can touch
Can you hear me?
I did as she told,
I could hear her, now.

She's really precious.
Like a cupcake.
I'll keep her in my pocket, forever.

12. Home

I'm at the bus stop
I feel the backpack weighing me down
I absentmindedly stare at the rush of vehicles in front of
me.

I have to cross the road,
They're waiting for me to come home,
I tell myself.
Or you could walk into the rush and that could be it
Nothing will weigh you down anymore,
My mind tells me.

What if things get better?
You can't do this to yourself
You'll regret it
You can't do this to them
You'll only pass the baton to them
The weight isn't going away just because you are
I tell myself.

The flashbacks from when I was bleeding, swamp me.
My eyes exude the pain of the past that is still present.
I reminisce yesterday— the voice, "You didn't do
anything when you were bleeding".

She didn't know I was much too drenched in the blood
for years
The blood I didn't carry until the past four years
Staying in tainted clothes for years does something
Something excruciatingly tormenting
More so when the clothes are sewn into your body
There was no water to wash my blood off
Even if I searched everywhere
All that was in my reach was to wait.
While the past gnaws on me until I'm achingly numb.

A vehicle honks
I wake up
Have faith,
I tell myself.

And you're not brave enough,
I chuckle to myself
Laugh it off in my head
I cross the road
Get into the car
She takes me home
They have me home
I owe them that
I owe the bleeding girl that
I'm home

It will get better, I tell myself.
It will get better.

The bleeding girl deserved to come home
I bled
But held on
Because she had to get home
Go home.

Poet's note:
To everyone who's in a place they don't want to be at,
hold on, please. When things get better, you don't want
to miss out on it, trust me. Even if the wait feels like
you're running in a circle. Hope is what one must have
when things are hard, anyone can hope for the best
when things are already sailing smoothly. It all comes
down to holding on when you're about to fall, that— is
faith.

13. Daylight

Cold sweats
Restlessness so numb
Screams so silent
I have a nightmare
I open my eyes
I see the nightmare
I'm living it
Only this time
I'm conscious
And I know I can't wake up in a night
But I know I'll wake up
I have to wake myself up
It has to be me
It's only me that is aware of the nightmare, in broad
daylight
I have me
I'll always have me
Wake up
It's only a nightmare

I might be broken
But I'm still here
Why didn't I disappear?
Because I can still heal

How did I not disappear?
I'm stronger than that.
I survived
And I'll continue living
Only I won't just survive
I'll thrive

I didn't choose the darkness
It took over
I choose daylight
It denies me
I deny it
But with time,
I will allow light
I choose light
I decide.

14. Older sister

An older sister—
She was mine
But she didn't have one

I was worried
How was it for you? I ask
She tells me.
I'm no longer worried.
I didn't know how
How did you do it? I ask
She tells me.
I now know.
I ponder over uncertainty
Will I get in? I ask
I don't know, I never think of losing, she tells me.
I no longer contemplate
I believe.
I have a test coming up,
She's written it before
Her notes
Her question papers
Her answers
She gives them all.

I'm nervous
You participated? I ask
I did, she tells me
How was it? I ask
She tells me.
I'm not nervous anymore.

I wonder more often as I grow up,
When she was the one asking questions
Whom did she go to?
What it was for her,
She made sure it was better for me.
She made my life easier.
I want to be there for her— forever,
Her younger sister.

15. Umbrella

An umbrella in the rain,
it finds it hard to approach the droplets.
But it finds itself elated when drenched.
For it finds true camaraderie, endearing.

As lonely as it is,
it wishes to be alone.
For every droplet that elaborates its loneliness,
as it cannot get inside,
it further opens itself,
shutting out every droplet.

Maybe a single droplet,
understanding it,
enveloping it in warmth,
as opposed to deepening its loneliness,
would lead to it closing its barrier.
To not shut out what drenches it,
It dreams to be drenched in what brought it warmth in
its dreams at night.
As the warmth it needs is not one that can be bought.

The loneliness hitherto does not change its desire for
warmth.

Until then,
it chooses being alone,
over loneliness that comes with the company of many.
It's alone, but not lonely.

16. While it lasted

I survived
She also survived
They withstood everything and everyone.

I survived them because I had her
She survived them because she had me
We had each other

She taught and I learnt
I taught and she learnt
We wrote our sorrows down in our notebooks
We read each other's pain.

All the daily routines in the last pages of our classworks,
We never followed through,
But I cherish the time that went into our planning.

"You read manhwas?"
We squealed with glee.
We bonded over your Mathematics
We bonded over my English
We bonded over what we wrote — feuds that anguished
us.
We bonded over Baymax and Tadashi Hamada

We bonded over animation
We bonded over yaoi
We bonded over acceptance
We bonded over maturity.

What changed us?
Your fear of losing irrelevant people
Your value of people who treated you horribly
Your choice of holding onto people who didn't deserve
you
Your choice of letting go of someone whom you bonded
with.

As I move on now,
Because I don't have it in me to fix toxicity, anymore
I was happy while it lasted.

17. Imprisoned

Imprisoned, I was.
Eyes, they bleed.
I, bleed.
Lips, they sleep.
I, sleep.

Underneath—
As I fade away,
What if it's only my face,
That remains.
I will hide,
Everything I am,
Beneath this face that remains.
Face that laughs,
Until it hurts,
Between the throat and neck,
The same place that hurts,
From restraining cries at 3 a.m.
The same face that smiles,
As everyone sees the face.
Is it really,
A smile?
Underneath.

Curtains—
They cover, they protect
Are they shielding what they're supposed to?
She's hiding,
A part of her is not.
Is she hiding because she bleeds?
Or is she bleeding because she's hiding?
The facades she bears,
What are they covering?
She cries,
But she has,
Curtains.

With every day,
With every class,
With every hour and twenty-five minutes,
With every minute,
With every second,
Is what I dread— dreadful?
It seems as though it is,
Yet I make it seem,
As though it isn't.
It is.
It is for me,
Whereas many chose,
So they do not dread.

Now—
Is not permanent
"I'm fine", she says.
She's just there,
That's all she is,
As of now.
Only as of now.
Now.

As stranded as I am in this prison,
I still am—
Because I know, I have a home,
To return to.
And for that, I am.
I am grateful.
Even when imprisoned.

18. Tired

Tired,
Tired of being called immature.
Tired,
Tired of being tired.
Tired,
Tired of hearing that I'm not tired.
Tired,
I'm tired.
Tired.

She said I was
Was I?
Maybe I was.

Immature
Am I?
Maybe I am.
Maybe I was never meant to grow up
Never meant to have opinions
Never meant to make my own decisions

Angry
I am.
Maybe I'm not allowed to be

Maybe I'm angry
Maybe it's because I'm immature
I'm angry,
So I'm immature?
Why does the goddess ever so wise and mature,
Spewing, "You're immature",
Have no other stance?
I'm immature,
And?

I am— tired
I am— immature? No.
I am— angry
So I am immature.

I speak words so I'm immature
I speak sentences so I'm immature
I talk— so I'm immature
I am immature.

I'm my own being,
So I'm immature
My emotions exist,
So I'm immature
I am immature.

19. Angel

Eyes like those of the sky's stars
Hair like those of the sea's agitated waves
Lips that drip like honey,
when she's at peace,
bringing me closer to solace.
There she was,
telling me it was all going to be okay,
though her lips wouldn't part an inch,
neither was there sound,
for there was comfort in our presence.
My angel, was she?

20. Voices

I'm trapped.
You're fine, I tell myself.
The voices get louder,
You did this to yourself, they say.
Make it stop, I scream.
Who are you screaming to?
There's no one here,
The voices say.

I reach for the headphones
I crank up the volume
Suddenly, I'm okay.
The voices stop,
Even if it's just for a moment.
I get them off of me,
After the silence worth a deep breath,
The voices are back.
I'm trapped again.

I go to bed.
The voices in my head are now as loud as they can be.
It will stop one day, I gulp down the fear of doubt.
One day— has arrived.
I'm not trapped anymore

I feel happiness seep in,
But I open my eyes
I'm awake
I'm trapped.

I'm better now,
I'm not trapped.
I might be trapped again,
But I will also be better again.
It all has to end.
Something else will start,
That will end too.
And then it starts.

21. Water

I want a flower
Flowers grow on trees and plants
Trees and plants grow through soil.
There is soil on Earth,
The Earth is where I must start.
But I continue asking for a flower
Am I even watering the tree?
Yes, I don't control the weather.
But is the weather the only one within my reach?
I can water the tree.

We want flowers but we aren't even watering our trees...
No, because fuck the weather that you can't control.
Water your tree.

You will find flowers, if you water the tree.
Water it,
Your flower will bloom one day.
Even if it doesn't, at least you won't regret not watering
it.
It would be the weather's fault.
You know what's scarier than failure?
Regrets.
So try.

Thorns might arise after,
Cut them,
Grab your flower.
Grow more flowers.

Find a flower you can love,
So watering doesn't come off as torturesome.
When you love the flower,
You want the flower,
You water the tree.

You love the flower; you love watering the tree.
The tree will grow— if you water it.

Water your tree,
To reap what you expect.
As you must expect,
And reap,
Only when you water your tree.

Water your tree,
And have faith in the weather.